PRAISE FOR DAVID AUBURN'S

PROOF

"A play about scientists whose science matters less than their humanity . . . All four [characters]—whether loving, hating, encouraging or impeding one another—are intensely alive, complex, funny, human." —JOHN SIMON, *New York*

"An exhilarating and assured new play . . . Accessible and compelling as a detective story."
—BRUCE WEBER, *The New York Times*

"Auburn has taken on some biggies here: what the link may be between genius and mental instability, why it is that lives get stuck, and how elusive the truth can be . . . [*Proof*'s] level of accomplishment and the realness of its characters show that Auburn has both depth and a voice."
—*The New Yorker*

"An exciting new drama . . . *Proof* . . . combines elements of mystery and surprise with old-fashioned storytelling to provide a compelling evening of theater."
—DAVID KAUFMAN, *New York Daily News*

DAVID AUBURN

THE COLUMNIST

David Auburn was born in Chicago and grew up in Ohio and Arkansas. He lives in New York City with his wife and two daughters.

ALSO BY DAVID AUBURN

Proof

THE
COLUMNIST

THE
COLUMNIST

A PLAY BY

DAVID AUBURN

FARRAR, STRAUS AND GIROUX

NEW YORK

Farrar, Straus and Giroux
18 West 18th Street, New York 10011

Copyright © 2012 by David Auburn
All rights reserved

Printed in the United States of America
First edition, 2012

Library of Congress Cataloging-in-Publication Data
Auburn, David, 1969–
The columnist : a play / by David Auburn. — 1st ed.
p. cm.
ISBN 978-0-86547-883-1 (alk. paper)
1. Alsop, Joseph, 1910–1989—Drama. I. Title.

PS3551.U28 C65 2012
812'.54—dc23
                                        2011047008

Designed by Jonathan D. Lippincott

www.fsgbooks.com

P1

TO FRAN

THE
COLUMNIST

Originally produced by the Manhattan Theatre Club, Lynne Meadow, Artistic Director; Barry Grove, Executive Producer. The first performance was on April 25, 2012.

Director	Daniel Sullivan
Set Design	John Lee Beatty
Costume Design	Jess Goldstein
Lighting Design	Kenneth Posner
Original Music and Sound Design	John Gromada
Projection Designer	Rocco DiSanti
Hair and Wig Designer	Charles LaPointe
Production Stage Manager	Jane Grey
Stage Manager	Denise Yaney

Cast of Characters

JOE ALSOP	John Lithgow
SUSAN MARY ALSOP	Margaret Colin
STEWART ALSOP	Boyd Gaines
ANDREI (YOUNG MAN, MAN)	Brian J. Smith
ABIGAIL	Grace Gummer
HALBERSTAM	Stephen Kunken
PHILIP	*Not yet cast as book went to press*

ACT ONE

SCENE 1

A hotel room. Moscow, 1954. JOE, *late forties, in bed. A* YOUNG MAN, *Russian, mid-twenties, getting dressed.*

JOE: Come back to bed.

YOUNG MAN: I have to go.

(*Beat.* JOE *watches him dress.*)

JOE: I've never had a Communist before.

YOUNG MAN: Can you tell the difference?

JOE: I'm not sure. I'd need to go again to give you a definitive answer.

YOUNG MAN: I'm giving a tour at four o'clock.

JOE: Where?

YOUNG MAN: Red Square.

JOE: That's down the block. We have plenty of time.

YOUNG MAN: This is my afternoon break. My boss does not like it when I'm gone so long.

JOE: Your "boss"?

YOUNG MAN: Is it the wrong word? For someone who tells you what to do?

JOE: It's the right word. I thought you were all comrades here.

YOUNG MAN: We are, yes. But he tells me what to do.

JOE: What if I told you to come back to bed?

YOUNG MAN: You are not my comrade.

JOE: No, I'm your superior. I'm older than you and American and I have more money. Now do as I say.

YOUNG MAN: Go to hell.

(JOE *chuckles, lights a cigarette.*)

JOE: Your English is extremely good, you know that?

YOUNG MAN: I was sent to government language schools. I do tours in French and German also.

JOE: Do you have a family?

YOUNG MAN: A sister.

JOE: What does she do?

YOUNG MAN: She's a laundress.

JOE: Doesn't have your talent for languages.

YOUNG MAN: She was a great athlete.

JOE: Really? What sort?

YOUNG MAN: Skiing. She tried out for the national team. As a girl. She was nearly chosen.

JOE: Good for her.

YOUNG MAN: We had interviews with the sports officials. Quite an exciting time. They took us to dinner, breakfasts in hotels with other athletes and their families. Eggs, sausages, fresh tomatoes, coffee with cream, thick white bread. Then she had a disappointing race, and . . .

JOE: What happened?

YOUNG MAN: Well, the meals stopped. We had been given a new refrigerator. Men came and took it away. They didn't even bring the old one back. We had to use the neighbor's from across the hall for five months—they let us have one shelf. Finally, finally, we got another refrigerator, an old one, worse than the one we started with.

JOE: No, I meant, what happened at the race?

YOUNG MAN: What do you mean, what happened?

JOE: Well, did she fall on the course, or—

YOUNG MAN: No, she didn't fall. She ran a good course. She just came a bit short of the required time is all. She was nervous. How would you feel?

JOE: That's awful.

(*Beat.*)

YOUNG MAN: What is your job?

JOE: I'm a journalist.

YOUNG MAN: That's why you ask me so many questions.

JOE: I suppose so.

YOUNG MAN: Are you from New York?

JOE: Washington.

YOUNG MAN: Which is your newspaper?

JOE: Oh, I'm in hundreds.

YOUNG MAN: Hundreds?

JOE: Well. A hundred and ninety, at last count. I have a syndicated column. With my brother.

YOUNG MAN: How many newspapers do you have in America?

JOE: I don't know. Thousands, I suppose.

YOUNG MAN: No.

JOE: Easily. Every major city has five or six. Morning,

afternoon, evening. Even the smallest town has its own weekly. It's one of our great strengths.

YOUNG MAN: You write one thing, one "column," it goes into one hundred and ninety newspapers.

JOE: Yes.

YOUNG MAN: And each of them pays you.

JOE: Yes.

YOUNG MAN: Are you rich?

JOE: Yes, by your standards.

YOUNG MAN: I'm beginning to think I should stay after all.

JOE: I won't pay you. That would tip things over into the sordid.

YOUNG MAN: I was joking. Don't insult me.

JOE: Sorry.

(*Beat.*)

YOUNG MAN: So, what are you writing about here?

JOE: The menace you pose to us.

YOUNG MAN: Me?

JOE: You seem very nice. No, you collectively.

YOUNG MAN: And your readers in a hundred and ninety newspapers, this is what they want to read? How scary we are?

JOE: We don't give two shits what they want to read. We tell them what they need to know.

YOUNG MAN: You and your brother. Is he here too?

JOE: We never travel together. One of us goes, one of us stays home and writes, we switch off . . . Now you seem to be asking me all the questions.

YOUNG MAN: Maybe I should be a journalist. If we had more than one newspaper. And journalists.

JOE: (*Laughs*) Tell me something. Why on earth do they have you doing tours? An intelligent young man like you, with your languages . . . Why aren't you in, I don't know, the diplomatic corps?

YOUNG MAN: I have wondered this myself, very often. I applied once. I was rejected.

JOE: They don't tell you why?

YOUNG MAN: No. Maybe something to do with my sister, I don't know.

JOE: And you have no appeal in the matter?

YOUNG MAN: Of course not.

JOE: Barbaric country. You'd like America.

YOUNG MAN: I would like to go there. It's impossible, of course.

JOE: Someday, when your Soviet masters give up on this idiotic "experiment" and rejoin the civilized world— assuming, of course, we haven't already blasted each other into clouds of radioactive vapor—you can come, and I'll show you Washington.

YOUNG MAN: How would you introduce me? To your friends?

JOE: As my linguist.

YOUNG MAN: Are you free in America? More than here?

JOE: Oh my God, yes. Are you joking?

YOUNG MAN: I mean, about this.

(*He indicates the two of them, the bed.*)

9

JOE: Oh. No. With that it's much the same.

(*Beat.*)

YOUNG MAN: I'd like to see Washington. And the Grand Canyon.

JOE: Not convenient to one another, unfortunately, but they should both be seen, and in the company of a knowledgeable guide. The Grand Canyon I don't know much about, but nobody knows Washington like me. It's my territory. Everyone knows me, everyone fears me, so if you're with me, you are guaranteed a good table at restaurants.

YOUNG MAN: Why do they fear you?

JOE: I simply have a well-deserved reputation for speaking my mind, loudly. Have you heard of Joe McCarthy?

YOUNG MAN: The fellow who says everyone in America is a Communist? We like him.

JOE: Yes, well, he's a contemptible thug and liar and a drunk, and he's causing considerable havoc right now. Everyone's quaking in fear of him. Except Stewart and me. We've been going after McCarthy with all guns blazing. Probably we're the only ones who could get away with it.

YOUNG MAN: I don't care very much about politics.

JOE: My boy, politics is life! Politics is human intercourse at its most sublimely ridiculous and intensely vital. You may as well say you don't care very much for sex.

YOUNG MAN: No, that I like.

JOE: Yes, I've noticed. Can't you spare me half an hour more?

YOUNG MAN: No, I'm sorry. I'm late already.

(YOUNG MAN *goes into the bathroom.*)

JOE: Have you ever been with an American before?

YOUNG MAN: (*From off*) No.

JOE: How do you know Atkinson?

YOUNG MAN: Atkinson?

JOE: The PAO.

YOUNG MAN: I'm sorry?

JOE: The Public Affairs Officer. At the embassy.

(YOUNG MAN *comes back in.*)

YOUNG MAN: Your embassy?

JOE: Yes.

YOUNG MAN: I'm sorry, I don't know him.

JOE: But he told me about you.

YOUNG MAN: I don't know what you're talking about.

JOE: He told me that he'd take care of things. He's—well, he's like us, you see.

(YOUNG MAN *shakes his head.*)

JOE: I told him I was hoping to find some company for to-night. And he said he'd help. Peter *Atkinson*. At the United States Embassy. Quite tall, reddish hair thinning a bit . . .

YOUNG MAN: I don't know this man. I met you in the bar.

JOE: You came right up to me. I assumed Peter sent you.

YOUNG MAN: You offered to buy me a drink.

JOE: And you accepted so *readily*.

YOUNG MAN: Why should I not accept?

JOE: Well, because you're so young, and . . . and I'm . . . You can't blame me for assuming . . .

YOUNG MAN: My God. You thought I was . . . *procured* for you?

JOE: Your English really is splendid.

YOUNG MAN: Picked out for you? Like a prostitute? Is this the arrangement you have with your *embassy*?

JOE: No, my God no, it's nothing *official*. Peter's an old friend and he's discreet and knows a man can get lonely in a foreign city. I ask for a warm body, he finds one.

YOUNG MAN: A warm body?

JOE: Oh dear. That doesn't sound right. Look, I'm just a bit confused—

YOUNG MAN: We had a conversation! I thought you were interested in what I had to say. Every day at work, I take the tourists around, I recite for them the history of this church or square, oh, Pushkin lived here, or Catherine the Great built this, and the great Soviet experiment . . . You, in the bar, were the first one to ask about *me*. I've never been asked so many questions in my life.

JOE: And you didn't give me a single answer.

YOUNG MAN: Not in public. I don't want to be arrested. But the effort I appreciated.

JOE: I want to make sure I understand this correctly. Are you saying you came here because you *wanted* to?

YOUNG MAN: Yes.

(*Beat.*)

JOE: I'm sorry. I'm not at all used to this.

YOUNG MAN: What's the matter?

JOE: Nothing.

YOUNG MAN: Are you all right?

JOE: Yes, of course.

YOUNG MAN: I have to leave now.

JOE: I don't know your name.

YOUNG MAN: It's Andrei.

JOE: Andrei. I'm Joe.

ANDREI: Yes, I know. Joe Alsop.

JOE: How do you know?

ANDREI: You said.

JOE: Did I?

ANDREI: When we met in the bar. I have a very good memory.

JOE: Did you know who I was?

ANDREI: No. But I will look for you in the newspaper from now on.

JOE: How can you read my columns over here?

ANDREI: I can't. But when *Pravda* denounces your columns, I will say, Yes! Joe! I knew him.

JOE: Wonderful. I should like that.

(*They shake hands, awkwardly.*)

And thank you for . . . the loveliest afternoon I've had in a long, long time.

(JOE *holds* ANDREI's *hand. Beat.*)

ANDREI: I have to go.

JOE: Of course, of course.

(ANDREI *exits. Beat.* JOE *begins to get dressed. After a moment, a knock at the door.* JOE *starts. He goes to the door.*)

Andrei?

VOICE: (*Off*) Mr. Alsop?

JOE: (*Disappointed*) Yes?

VOICE: We would like to speak with you, please.

JOE: Who is it?

VOICE: Just let us in, Mr. Alsop.

(JOE *hesitates, then starts to open the door.*)

fade

SCENE 2

JOE's *house in Georgetown. January 1961.* STEWART *(late forties) in a tuxedo. He looks tired. Puts his feet up. Lights a cigarette. Loosens his tie.* SUSAN MARY *enters. Forties, attractive. Robe and slippers. They look at each other, surprised.*

SUSAN MARY: Hello.

STEWART: Hi. Joe said to come over.

SUSAN MARY: Is Tish here?

STEWART: Home with the kids.

(Beat. He looks at her.)

SUSAN MARY: What?

STEWART: Nothing.

SUSAN MARY: You're surprised.

STEWART: A little.

SUSAN MARY: He hasn't said anything.

STEWART: About what?

SUSAN MARY: No. I'd better let him tell you.

STEWART: Why?

SUSAN MARY: He's your brother.

STEWART: He really tells me very little.

SUSAN MARY: Yes, well, he's going to tell you to get your feet off his coffee table.

STEWART: What is this? It looks pretty fancy.

SUSAN MARY: It's eighteenth-century. He's been going to auctions. Do you want something to drink?

STEWART: Don't go to any trouble. I can help myself.

SUSAN MARY: It's no trouble.

(JOE *enters.*)

JOE: There you are. I was afraid you went to bed.

SUSAN MARY: Tonight? No. Are we expecting anyone else?

JOE: Not to my knowledge. There should be some champagne chilling; bring it in here, would you, my dear?

SUSAN MARY: Mmm-hmm.

(*She goes.* STEWART *looks at* JOE.)

JOE: She keeps a dressing gown here, and some comfortable shoes, for late nights. I shouldn't let her?

STEWART: Just never known you to share the house with anyone.

JOE: It's hardly sharing the *house*. She's here two or three nights a week as it is, for parties. She's an ideal hostess. I have to have *someone* at the foot of the table. Especially now. My God, socially this place is going to become *electrifying*. Don't smoke that.

(*He takes the cigarette out of* STEWART's *mouth.*)

STEWART: Hey—

JOE: Smoke this.

(*Gives him a cigar.* STEWART *examines it.*)

STEWART: Wow. Thanks. Inside?

JOE: Tonight, yes.

STEWART: You are feeling good.

JOE: He's our kind of man, Stewart.

STEWART: He's the Irish Catholic son of a bootlegger.

JOE: That sort of thing doesn't matter to you. You know what I mean. Jack will make this country interesting again, but more importantly, he'll make the *town* interesting again. He's got that gleam in the eye that FDR had. I didn't realize how much I'd missed it. Eisenhower was so plodding and dreary. His Washington was like going to bed with a glass of warm milk and a woman in curlers.

STEWART: That's not bad. Have you used it?

JOE: It's all yours.

STEWART: Everyone would know it was you.

JOE: Kennedy . . . Kennedy's Veuve Clicquot, and a starlet on each arm. And one of them has a degree from the Sorbonne.

STEWART: That one needs work.

JOE: Oh, stop affecting nonchalance. You feel the same way I do.

STEWART: I just don't think we should get carried away.

JOE: I do. I will. This one night, I will be carried away, and so will you, goddamn it. Only, get your feet off my coffee table. It's eighteenth-century. Or at least take off your shoes— Oh, never mind. You know what? Put your feet up. Stand on the sofa, do whatever you want tonight.

STEWART: I want to go to bed.

JOE: Then you're a fool. How many nights do we get like this? He's *our man*. A tough man and a thoughtful one too, the kind we've been dreaming of and waiting for. He's like Stevenson with balls. Brains and balls, finally, in one package! And beauty. And charm. And he owes us.

STEWART: Does he?

JOE: You're damn right he does. The "missile gap"—we gave that to him on a plate; hell, you *named* it, and he beat Nixon to death with it.

STEWART: He barely squeaked by.

JOE: All the more reason, then. Without me pushing the Johnson pick and the missile gap pieces, he might well have fallen short. And don't think he doesn't know it. Don't think he won't remember that debt either, and repay it, because that's the sort of man he is.

STEWART: We'll see.

JOE: Yes we will. We're going to see *everything*. We're in an extraordinary position, Stew, at an extraordinary time, this is *our moment*, so why do you look so goddamn depressed? Go home if you're not going to celebrate with me, for Chrissake.

STEWART: I'm just tired.

JOE: You have no sense of history.

STEWART: I have enough of a sense of history to know that when a man in a tuxedo smoking a cigar announces "This is our moment," he's generally fucked.

JOE: Then here's to being fucked. It's a new day, Stew. We should revive the partnership.

STEWART: What?

JOE: Why not? Come back to the column. The Alsop brothers. Together again. What do you say?

STEWART: "No."

JOE: Foolish. Shortsighted.

STEWART: I'm happy at the *Post*.

JOE: *The Saturday Evening Post*. It's in decline. Becoming pablum for salesmen and housewives. Don't you want to write for the people who matter?

STEWART: I think housewives matter.

JOE: Don't be sentimental.

STEWART: I get to write nice long pieces at the *Post* and the editors mostly stay out of my way. Okay, I don't have the impact I did when we wrote together . . .

JOE: So why wouldn't you want to come back?

STEWART: Because you're such a colossal pain in the ass.

JOE: Yes, but what else?

STEWART: You never paid me enough. Actually, I was never sure why *you* paid *me* at all.

JOE: We'll go sixty–forty this time.

STEWART: That's mighty generous, Joe.

JOE: Fifty-five–forty-five. That's fair—you can keep your contract with the *Post*; the column is all I have.

STEWART: I've got a family to support.

JOE: So have I.

STEWART: Who?

JOE: Susan. And her daughter.

STEWART: What?

JOE: We're getting married.

STEWART: When?

JOE: Next month.

(*Beat.*)

STEWART: Congratulations.

JOE: Thank you. I asked her last March, you know, and she turned me down. My fault; it was too soon after Bill's death. Then, after Jack got the nomination, I suppose I was emboldened and I asked her again, and she said yes.

STEWART: That's terrific, Joe. I'm happy for you.

JOE: I'm happy for me. I can't believe my luck, honestly. She's everything I want. She's sparkling and bright and at home in the world. And she'll fit in here, beautifully. She already does. And her daughter has become very dear to me.

STEWART: I should have seen this coming.

JOE: Surely it can't be that much of a surprise. We've been friends for years.

STEWART: I didn't realize you'd become more than friends.

JOE: I didn't either, until suddenly I did.

STEWART: And does she . . .

JOE: Of course. I told her myself. In a letter.

STEWART: What did she say?

JOE: It's not a major concern. You haven't given me an answer. The column.

STEWART: I thought I did. Not in a million years.

JOE: You haven't given me a reason.

STEWART: Okay. Apart from the money . . . and the

abuse . . . and the general indignity of working for my big brother at the age of forty-six . . . I guess I just like where I am.

JOE: The Norman Rockwell Weekly.

STEWART: On the outside.

JOE: Why on earth would you want to be *there?*

STEWART: I guess I think that's where a reporter belongs.

JOE: That's *profoundly* wrong. You realize that, I hope. That is the stupidest goddamn thing I have ever heard in my *life.* Forget it. I rescind the offer.

(SUSAN MARY *enters with a bottle of champagne and glasses. She's changed out of the robe.*)

SUSAN MARY: There's a tub of ice in the kitchen. It's filled with bottles.

JOE: Yes, I asked Jose to set some to chill.

SUSAN MARY: He's brought up a case from the basement. How much are you planning on celebrating tonight?

JOE: To excess.

STEWART: Congratulations.

SUSAN MARY: Here's to the President.

STEWART: I'm drinking to you.

SUSAN MARY: Good. You told him. (JOE *nods. To* STEWART) We weren't going to announce it until after the inauguration.

JOE: We didn't want to hog the limelight from Jack.

SUSAN MARY: He's joking.

STEWART: I'm not sure he was.

JOE: Oh, fuck you, Stew, of course I was.

SUSAN MARY: Joe.

JOE: Sorry.

(*She gives* STEWART *a sympathetic look.*)

SUSAN MARY: Well, I guess I'd better do my part. (*She takes a glass.*) Shouldn't you tell Jose we don't need so much?

JOE: We may have visitors.

SUSAN MARY: It's two in the morning, Joe.

JOE: The balls are just letting out.

SUSAN MARY: Who did you invite?

JOE: No one.

SUSAN MARY: Are we having a party or not?

JOE: If people drop in for a drink, on this *historic* evening, I want to be prepared. You never know who might want a nightcap.

SUSAN MARY: Oh God. This is my life now, isn't it? I was going to have a hot bath.

JOE: The hell you were. (*To* STEWART) She stays up later than I do. I never met a woman more enamored of the social whirl.

SUSAN MARY: I thought you were the one who wanted to get home. (*To* STEWART) We couldn't get a cab on Pennsylvania Avenue. He was in absolute hysterics.

JOE: It was snowing. I was cold. Was I that bad?

SUSAN MARY: You were awful. *Screaming—*

JOE: I was not screaming.

SUSAN MARY: All right, ranting.

JOE: What if our guests had beat me home?

SUSAN MARY: Aha. You hear that? What guests?

JOE: No one. In particular. People may stop by, is all.

SUSAN MARY: If anyone were coming, they'd have been here by now. (*To* STEWART) He can't stand to think his house isn't the center of the universe tonight.

JOE: Wherever *you* are, my dear, is the center of *my* universe, and I would be perfectly happy were it just the three of us tonight, but I have laid in supplies just in case.

STEWART: Well, I want to go to bed.

JOE: Yes, you've made that very clear. Go, then. You'll miss out.

SUSAN MARY: On what?

(ABIGAIL, *fourteen, enters.*)

ABIGAIL: What's going on? Are you having a party?

JOE: Yes.

SUSAN MARY: No. We're just saying good night. Go back to bed.

JOE: Do not go back to bed. Stew, you know Susan's daughter-soon-to-be-my-stepdaughter, Abigail? Abigail, my brother Stewart.

STEWART: Hello.

ABIGAIL: Hi. Do I call him Uncle Stewart?

JOE: No.

STEWART: She can if she wants.

ABIGAIL: Can I have some champagne?

SUSAN MARY: No.

JOE: Of course. (*Goes to pour it.*) In fact, you must. I don't understand why you were even in bed—

SUSAN MARY: It's the middle of the night. (*To* STEWART) We've been staying here during the week . . . it's closer to her school . . .

ABIGAIL: I've got an exam tomorrow.

JOE: An *exam*? They give you an exam the morning after the *inauguration*? How are they supposed to concentrate?

ABIGAIL: I don't know. Half the girls' parents were going to parties. Some of the girls were having their *own* parties.

SUSAN MARY: At fourteen. Isn't that ridiculous?

ABIGAIL: You're so stodgy.

JOE: She certainly is.

SUSAN MARY: One's at a hotel. With an orchestra. We got an engraved invitation. Can you imagine? They're children.

ABIGAIL: You're supposed to go dressed like Jackie. They got a singer who sounds *exactly* like Nat King Cole. I can't believe I'm missing it.

SUSAN MARY: Imagine. Buying Chanel suits for fourteen-year-old girls.

ABIGAIL: You could have loaned me one of yours.

SUSAN MARY: Over my dead body.

JOE: And your pearls. The long strand.

ABIGAIL: Oh, the long strand!

SUSAN MARY: (*To* JOE) Stop causing trouble. Go to bed, Abby. Don't give her that, Joe, she's going to be exhausted.

JOE: Champagne is revitalizing.

STEWART: That is not actually true.

(JOE *gives* ABIGAIL *a glass of champagne.*)

JOE: What's the exam?

ABIGAIL: Latin.

SUSAN MARY: It's her worst subject.

JOE: Not for long. I happen to be a fervent and dedicated Latinist. I can still give you *reams* of Virgil. Won all the prizes at Groton.

STEWART: That *is* true.

JOE: I helped Stew.

STEWART: Got a D in Latin. Would have been an F without him.

JOE: Which established the template for the rest of his career. I've been all that's standing between him and humiliating failure for twenty years.

STEWART: Oh, fuck you, Joe. (*Beat. To* ABIGAIL) Excuse me.

SUSAN MARY: It's all right.

STEWART: I'm very sorry.

SUSAN MARY: It's not your fault. Honestly, Joe.

JOE: (*Mild*) Sorry. (*Indicates his glass.*) High spirits. Anyway. We'll have your marks up in no time. You will find me a patient if relentless instructor. We shall commence daily tutorials in the first full day of the Kennedy administration. Now drink.

(ABIGAIL *looks to her mother, who nods.* ABIGAIL *drinks.*)

SUSAN MARY: Stewart, now, about the wedding. Don't say anything to Tish. I want to tell her myself. Promise?

STEWART: Of course. What kind of thing are you planning?

JOE: We haven't discussed the actual event yet—

SUSAN MARY: And *we* won't be discussing it. I'm handling it, thanks, and it'll be simple, simple.

JOE: I'm in your hands.

SUSAN MARY: Good.

STEWART: You are a very lucky man. You—

(ABIGAIL *has drained her glass.*)

ABIGAIL: My teacher says Kennedy's all flash.

JOE: What?

ABIGAIL: That he's just a lucky pretty boy who gets by on charm and his daddy's money.

STEWART: What sort of Latin teacher is this?

JOE: No wonder you're failing. The man sounds like a boob.

ABIGAIL: She's a woman.

JOE: Let me guess. Sixtyish. Mannish hands. Trace of a mustache. Flask in her desk drawer. Virgin, possibly lesbian.

SUSAN MARY: Joe—

JOE: Voted for Wendell Willkie.

ABIGAIL: Who's Wendell Willkie?

JOE: My God, Susan, what sort of education is this child receiving?

STEWART: Who's the first president you remember?

ABIGAIL: Truman.

JOE: Really?

SUSAN MARY: She was born in 1946, Joe.

JOE: So more or less your entire political consciousness, your understanding of the modern presidency itself, has been shaped by . . . *Dwight Eisenhower?*

ABIGAIL: I guess so.

JOE: Oh, you poor child. Come, sit with Uncle Joe. Have some more champagne. (*Before* SUSAN MARY *can say "No"*) Yes. You cannot imagine how different this city was when I first came in the late 1930s. You could hardly call it a city. It was a town. Everybody knew each other. A young reporter knew everyone, every senator, every cabinet head. I knew everyone, and not because of family connections, either. It was a town. People knew you walking down the street. Cousin Eleanor invited us to the White House for scrambled eggs. Her scrambled eggs were appalling, really dreadful, but she made them herself, and the President mixed the martinis and handed them around, and that's how business was done, and you talked and laughed and learned and listened, and there was a marvelous sense of excitement and of new beginnings. And now—you have the enormous good fortune to be living in the same sort of era. The city's changed, of course. Air-conditioning, and real restaurants, and the gray hordes of staff and lobbyists rumbling about night and day, everything's more complicated . . . Jackie won't be serving scrambled eggs—thank *God*, it's going to be infinitely more glamorous and sophisticated . . . but once again it's a time of youth and excitement and energy; "vigor," as our new man in the White House likes to say. He's going to do marvelous things, you shall see. Oh, there will be setbacks, and disappointments. I'm sure we'll have our hearts broken sixteen different ways, and when that happens we'll let the White House know, *I'll* let them know; believe me, we won't be soft on them. Good friends don't withhold criticism when it's warranted. But watch. Jack understands the Soviets.

He'll know how to deal with them. He'll do something about civil rights. He'll do something about Indochina. (*To* STEWART) That's coming—you watch. The Communists will keep the pressure on, they'll keep testing us, in Laos—

STEWART: Not Laos.

JOE: No, perhaps not, but possibly—or possibly Vietnam . . . and Jack will do what needs to be done. And if he doesn't *know* what needs to be done, I'll tell him. Or if he knows but wavers, he will hear from me then too. (*To* STEWART) And he could be hearing from *you*, if you had any sense. Fifty–fifty? My name would still come first, it's alphabetical . . .

(STEWART *looks at* JOE. *Beat. He puts down his glass.*)

STEWART: Good night, everyone. (*He kisses* SUSAN MARY.) Congratulations again.

SUSAN MARY: Thank you.

(*The phone rings.* SUSAN MARY *goes to answer it.*)

STEWART: (*To* ABIGAIL) I'm sorry you missed your parties. There'll be others.

ABIGAIL: I know.

(STEWART *exits.*)

SUSAN MARY: Hello? I'm sorry? (*To* JOE) It's for you. It's the Secret Service.

JOE: What? (JOE *takes the phone.*) Hello?

(STEWART *comes back in.*)

STEWART: What the hell's going on outside? There's a crowd across the street, there's a gang of photographers on the sidewalk—

(JOE *shushes him.*)

JOE: (*On phone*) Yes. No, I understand. Well, thank you very much for calling.

STEWART: I can't get out the goddamn door.

JOE: (*To* SUSAN MARY) Bring in a few more bottles. (*To* ABIGAIL) You may want to change your clothes.

fade

SCENE 3

A bar in Saigon. September 1963. STEWART *with a glass of beer.* HALBERSTAM *(late twenties) approaches him. He carries a sheet of teletype paper.*

HALBERSTAM: I heard you were in town.

STEWART: I just got in yesterday.

HALBERSTAM: Good of you to join us.

STEWART: Thanks. Have we met?

HALBERSTAM: Halberstam. The *Times*.

STEWART: I read your stuff. Good to meet you. Stew Alsop.
(*Beat.*)

HALBERSTAM: I looked for you over at the Caravelle.

STEWART: This is more my kind of place.

HALBERSTAM: Mine too. Wouldn't drink the beer, though.

STEWART: Tastes okay to me.

HALBERSTAM: They don't wash the glasses. You need something stronger if you want to kill the hepatitis.

(STEWART *smiles.*)

STEWART: Can I get us both something?

HALBERSTAM: No, thanks. What are you working on?

STEWART: Piece for the *Post*.

HALBERSTAM: Fine paper.

STEWART: *The Saturday Evening Post.*

HALBERSTAM: Oh. Well. They publish some good things.

STEWART: We sneak it in, when we can. Between the recipes.

HALBERSTAM: State of the conflict, that kind of thing? "Turning back the Red Tide . . ."

STEWART: Depends on what I see, I suppose.

HALBERSTAM: Uh-huh. Who's showing you around?

STEWART: I'm finding my own way around.

HALBERSTAM: Good for you.

STEWART: Thanks.

HALBERSTAM: Not like your brother.

STEWART: Sorry?

HALBERSTAM: He was just in town last week.

STEWART: I wasn't aware.

HALBERSTAM: You guys don't travel together?

STEWART: No. Why would we?

HALBERSTAM: I thought—

STEWART: Why were you looking for me at the Caravelle, Mr. Halberstam?

HALBERSTAM: I was . . . delegated.

STEWART: By whom?

HALBERSTAM: By my colleagues. After we read Joe's latest column. We get it a little late over here, when *Stars and Stripes* picks it up, but some of the wire service guys made sure I saw this one right away. I dunno, maybe I should be flattered . . .

STEWART: You'll have to help me out. I haven't read it.

HALBERSTAM: Don't you guys work together?

STEWART: Not formally, not for a long time.

HALBERSTAM: But informally?

STEWART: Mr. Halberstam, if my brother wrote something that's bothering you—

HALBERSTAM: He blames *us*.

STEWART: For what?

HALBERSTAM: For everything. The whole situation here. He blames *us*, his fellow reporters. And here I thought we were all in the same business.

STEWART: As I say, I haven't read it, but I'm sure he doesn't mean to—

HALBERSTAM: (*Reads*) "The constant pressure of the reportorial crusade against the Vietnamese government"— that's me and my colleagues, if I'm not mistaken—"has helped mightily"—mightily!—"to transform Diem from a courageous quite viable national leader into a man afflicted with galloping persecution mania, seeing plots around every corner."

STEWART: Joe wrote this?

(HALBERSTAM *hands him the paper. Beat.*)

STEWART: I see.

HALBERSTAM: *We* drove him crazy. The President of the country, the poor courageous, noble friend of the U.S., has been driven round the bend by assholes like me and the nasty things we write in American newspapers.

STEWART: This is new?

HALBERSTAM: It just came out. He must have filed it before he left the country.

STEWART: Maybe you should take it up with him.

HALBERSTAM: I'd like to, but he *left*. He's already gone.

STEWART: Well, I really don't see what you—

HALBERSTAM: He doesn't know the country, he breezes over here for a *week*, he stays with Lodge at the embassy, he gets his army car and driver, Westmoreland puts a helicopter at his disposal, he gets whatever he wants . . . Meanwhile, the rest of us are killing ourselves here, worked to death, living in hovels, earning crap, eating crap, and taking literally *endless* shit back home for trying to tell a sliver of a fraction of the truth about this fucked-up place, and he saunters in with his pressed suits and his cigarette holder and his phony fucking Andover WASP Harvard accent, and his *connections* . . . and somehow manages to notice, during an exclusive *two-day* interview that the rest of us would give our eyeteeth for, that the fucking *head of the country*, the guy we're fighting and dying for, Our Man in Vietnam— who, by the way, you two have been cheerfully pimping from the get-go—he *notices* that this man is not only a corrupt and incompetent and hopeless loser and dope, as the rest of us have been saying for months if not years, but also, by the way, *actually insane*—He *notices* this . . . and then blames . . . the press! We did it! It's all our fault!

(*Beat.*)

STEWART: The accent's real.

HALBERSTAM: What?

STEWART: I don't think you can hold him responsible for that. It's how we were brought up.

HALBERSTAM: Is that all you have to say?

STEWART: Joe does know the country. He knows it very well.

HALBERSTAM: He was here for a *week*.

STEWART: He's been coming here since 1954. So have I. We covered Dien Bien Phu together. Joe's been coming to Asia since before the war. He was in a Japanese prison camp when you were in high school.

HALBERSTAM: Well, things have changed here since 1954.

STEWART: Yes. They washed the glasses then.

(HALBERSTAM *turns to go.*)

HALBERSTAM: Jesus. I knew there was no point.

STEWART: Just a moment. Let me make sure I understand. This column.

HALBERSTAM: Yes.

STEWART: Are you upset because you think Joe is describing you?

HALBERSTAM: He *is* describing me, and half a dozen other hardworking guys who are just trying to—

STEWART: No, he's not.

HALBERSTAM: Well, who the hell is it about, then?

STEWART: It's about you, but he's not describing you.

HALBERSTAM: What?

STEWART: Joe doesn't describe. That's what reporters do.

Joe's a columnist. He writes to effect. You see? There's your mistake. You're not in the same business at all.

HALBERSTAM: Yeah, well, we are not the enemy! I don't have to take this shit. I'm gonna send a cable.

STEWART: To who?

HALBERSTAM: My editor. He's got friends at the *Post*. Not your *Post*, the good one. He can call them. He can stick up for his staff for once.

STEWART: What difference will that make?

HALBERSTAM: It—

STEWART: This is not a fight between you and Joe. Joe's playing on a different field. The same things Joe's writing in his column, he's telling Kennedy in person.

HALBERSTAM: Bullshit.

STEWART: (*Checks his watch.*) He's probably with him now, patiently explaining that, after a thorough investigation, he can say with confidence that except for the little problem of Diem we are on the right track in Vietnam, and you kids over here who say differently are juvenile, deluded malcontents. At *best*.

HALBERSTAM: He can just waltz into the Oval Office and talk to Kennedy.

STEWART: You know where Kennedy went on inauguration night? After all the balls, after Jackie went home to rest, when he just wanted to relax, get a little drunk, his first night as President? He went to Joe's house. I was there.

(*Beat.*)

HALBERSTAM: Yeah, well, Kennedy doesn't run the fucking assignment desk at *The New York Times*.

STEWART: David, take my advice. Don't go picking fights with Joe Alsop.

HALBERSTAM: Joe Alsop is a fucking prima donna who's giving us all a bad name, and it's time for somebody to push back against the little queer.

(*Beat.*)

STEWART: Excuse me?

HALBERSTAM: I'm sorry. I . . . But everybody knows. He uses a *cigarette holder,* for Chrissake.

STEWART: My brother is a very happily married man.

HALBERSTAM: Oh come on, Stewart. I'm sorry, but every- body knows about the pictures.

STEWART: I don't have any idea what you're talking about.

HALBERSTAM: I know guys who've seen them.

(*Beat.*)

STEWART: Who?

HALBERSTAM: People. They've circulated. A bit.

STEWART: But *you* haven't seen them. These "pictures."

HALBERSTAM: It's a well-known thing. It's . . . newspaper lore. The roll of film from the Moscow hotel room . . . The great Cold Warrior who got set up and blackmailed by the KGB. It's why he's so strident now, he knows he's compromised.

(STEWART *considers this calmly.*)

STEWART: Who do you know that's seen them?

HALBERSTAM: I've heard from a bunch of different people. FBI guys, mostly.

STEWART: "FBI guys."

HALBERSTAM: Evidently Hoover has the negatives.

STEWART: And you believe that?

HALBERSTAM: I . . . it . . .

STEWART: The KGB sends its dirty photos to Hoover.

HALBERSTAM: No, but—

STEWART: My brother's "compromised," so he's *harder* on the Soviets?

Gossip. Spiteful, envious sleaze that doesn't even make sense on its face. I thought you were a better reporter than that. (STEWART *puts down his drink.*) Do you know, for a moment there I was actually going to defend you to Joe? But now I think I'd better just say good afternoon, and go fuck yourself.

fade

SCENE 4

JOE's *study. November 1963.* ABIGAIL *(now sixteen) in a chair with schoolbooks on her lap.* JOE *perched on his desk.*

JOE: Again.

ABIGAIL: *Dividimus muros et moenia pandimus urbis. Accingunt omnes operum, pedibusque rotarum subiciunt lapsus, et stuppea vincula collo intendunt: scandit fatalis machina muros, feta armes.*

JOE: Very good. Only it's *operi* not *operum*, and *armis* not *armes.* But otherwise, you're doing splendidly.

ABIGAIL: *(Packing up her books)* Thanks, Joe.

JOE: Where are you going? We have to review your vocabulary.

ABIGAIL: Not today.

JOE: Yes, today. Don't you have a quiz Friday?

ABIGAIL: Yeah, but I'll do fine.

JOE: Last week you got a B. I think we could do a little better than that.

ABIGAIL: But I have to be somewhere at two.

JOE: Where?

ABIGAIL: Somewhere.

JOE: Where?

ABIGAIL: Joe. Come on.

JOE: I have not tutored you assiduously for the past two years to watch you slack off now. I had to reschedule or postpone *multiple* important interviews to preserve today's session. Shall I read you the list?

ABIGAIL: No.

JOE: Two United States congressmen. An undersecretary of defense. A top Senate staffer. The First Lady of the United States.

ABIGAIL: What?

JOE: You heard me.

ABIGAIL: You canceled with *Jackie* to help me practice my Latin vocab.

JOE: Yes.

ABIGAIL: Liar.

JOE: Prove it.

ABIGAIL: They're not even in town. I read about it.

JOE: Very good. The others were real; that last was an exaggeration designed to suggest the importance I attach to your education.

ABIGAIL: Thanks, but don't bullshit me, Joe.

JOE: I take it back. You have learned some new vocabulary.

ABIGAIL: You use language like that all the time.

JOE: I am not a fifteen-year-old girl.

ABIGAIL: Neither am I. I'm sixteen.

(*She gets up. She's wearing a skirt that stops above the knees.*)

JOE: Dear God. What are you wearing?

ABIGAIL: What? Nothing.

JOE: I can see that. Were the bottom four inches torn off in some sort of garment-rending incident?

ABIGAIL: It's just a skirt. This is what people are wearing.

JOE: It's an abomination. It doesn't even cover your knees. Has your mother seen you in it?

ABIGAIL: What? I don't know. I guess.

JOE: Don't you dare leave the house like that. Where are you going, anyway?

ABIGAIL: None of your business.

JOE: A social occasion?

ABIGAIL: Maybe.

JOE: A date?

ABIGAIL: It's just a bunch of friends going out.

JOE: Male and female friends? That would account for the acres of calf you're exhibiting.

ABIGAIL: Oh, for God's sake—

(*The phone rings.*)

Better get that. Could be the Queen of England.

JOE: *Do not leave this room.* (*On phone*) Hello? Scotty! No, it's a perfectly good time, thanks for calling back. This won't take long. I just have one question and it's entirely public-spirited: When are you going to fire those irresponsible children you've got reporting for you in Southeast Asia?

Of course I'm serious.

If I didn't think it was an appropriate question, I wouldn't ask it. I—

(SUSAN MARY *enters.*)

Sorry, just a moment. *(To* SUSAN MARY*) Knock,* Susan. Is that really too much to ask? I'm working.

SUSAN MARY: I'm sorry, Joe. I just have a quick—

(JOE *holds up a hand to stop her.*)

JOE: I'm sorry, Scotty. I simply refuse to believe you and the paper wouldn't be far better off having them cover something more suited to their experience and abilities, such as high school athletics or one of the sleepier state legislatures . . .

SUSAN MARY: What are you wearing?

ABIGAIL: Nothing.

SUSAN MARY: You're not going out in that.

JOE: That's what I told her. Now, will you both please leave? I am trying to conduct a conversation.

ABIGAIL: A minute ago you ordered me to stay.

JOE: Now I am ordering you to go and change, and then come back for the rest of the lesson. Scotty, I'm sorry, I . . . Hello? Scotty?

(*He's lost the call.*)

Oh for God's sake, now look what's happened. Susan, really, I've asked not to be interrupted while I'm working.

SUSAN MARY: I thought you were having a lesson.

ABIGAIL: We're finished.

JOE: No, we still have to do your vocabulary. After you change your clothes.

SUSAN MARY: Yes, you really should change, Abby.

ABIGAIL: I can't believe you're siding with *him.*

SUSAN MARY: I'm not siding with anybody. You look very cute, but—

JOE: Cute? The outfit is an incitement to sexual assault.

SUSAN MARY: I do think the skirt is a little much. Especially for November.

ABIGAIL: My legs don't get cold! Please. Everyone gets to wear them out except me. My coat comes down past my knees, it doesn't matter anyway.

SUSAN MARY: If it doesn't matter, just put on a longer skirt.

ABIGAIL: Agh, I hate you both.

(ABIGAIL *stomps out.*)

SUSAN MARY: She's really become impossible.

JOE: Nonsense. She's just stretching her wings a bit. You shouldn't be so rigid.

SUSAN MARY: *I'm* rigid? You just said—

(JOE *is dialing the phone.*)

JOE: I am the stepparent. It's my job to be waspish and brutal, thus opening up the space for you to appear sympathetic and accommodating.

SUSAN MARY: You think I should let her wear the skirt?

JOE: She's right, they are all wearing them now, God help us. And she's worked awfully hard on her Latin. (*On the phone*) Yes. Joe Alsop for James Reston, please. We were accidentally disconnected.

SUSAN MARY: Joe, I wanted to talk to you about—

JOE: Susan, I'm on a phone call.

SUSAN MARY: A call you made after you knew I wanted to speak with you.

JOE: Can't it wait?

SUSAN MARY: It *can* wait, but I was hoping we could—

(JOE *holds his hand up.*)

JOE: Scotty. I'm sorry, I think we were accidentally disconnected. Well, why would you do that? (*Pause.*) All right, I'll tell you precisely where I get off calling the editor of a rival newspaper and telling him to fire his "star" reporters. First of all, I don't see us as "rivals"; that is a stupidly blinkered view of our business. We are all in this together and we have to look out for one another and for the greater journalistic good. Secondly, your boys over there—

They *are* boys, goddamn it, they *are* boys! Does Sheehan even have his driver's license? And if you let me know the date of Halberstam's bar mitzvah, I'll be sure to send him something nice—

Hello?

Shit.

(*He hangs up.*)

JOE: Susan, can we talk about this after dinner? I have an awful lot of work.

SUSAN MARY: It's about the trip.

JOE: Which trip?

SUSAN MARY: We talked about this. The London trip. Remember?

JOE: Oh. Yes. When are you going?

SUSAN MARY: We're going together, Joe.

JOE: When?

SUSAN MARY: That's what I'm here to— You really don't remember any of this.

JOE: No, of course I do. Just remind me of the reason?

SUSAN MARY: To see old friends. Abby has her winter break coming up, it'd be wonderful for her, *we've* never been . . .

JOE: Of course we've been.

SUSAN MARY: Not *together.* Don't you think it would be fun?

JOE: I'm sure it would be fun, and it's something we should definitely discuss.

SUSAN MARY: Good. Let's discuss it.

JOE: All right.

SUSAN MARY: All right.

(*Beat.*)

JOE: Is this the discussion?

SUSAN MARY: No, I don't think it is.

JOE: Well, what do you want me to do, book passage on the *Queen Mary* right now?

SUSAN MARY: We could talk about where we'd like to stay. You could look at your calendar. You could give me some dates that you have free—

JOE: Yes, well, there's the difficulty . . . I mean, it's very hard to imagine having any sort of break coming up. I've never been so swamped. Now, if you're talking about the summer, all right, but our dinners alone into New Year—

SUSAN MARY: We can cancel some of those.

JOE: Cancel?

SUSAN MARY: I'm not going to wait until the *summer*, Joe. I'm just talking about a little trip so we can spend some time together.

JOE: We're together every night.

SUSAN MARY: With a dozen or more guests.

JOE: With friends.

SUSAN MARY: Yes, and our *friends* will understand if we wanted to take a little break now and then.

JOE: But I don't want to take a little break.

SUSAN MARY: But I do. That's what I'm trying to tell you.

JOE: But you haven't said *why*.

SUSAN MARY: Yes, I have. Because there are other things I want to do.

JOE: My God, Susan, what else *have* you to do apart from sit at the end of my table and be fascinated by whatever is being said by the person on your right? How taxing can it be?

(*Beat.*)

SUSAN MARY: It's a pleasure. And a privilege. That I wish to forgo. For a few weeks of travel with my husband and daughter. How taxing could *that* be?

JOE: Oh, now you're being ridiculous. If we can't discuss this rationally, there's no point. Honestly, you surprise me. This is my work. Our work. This is what we do, you know that. Go and have a nap.

(*The phone rings.* JOE *waits for her to go.*)

SUSAN MARY: I'm not through with you.

(SUSAN MARY *exits.* JOE *answers.*)

JOE: How dare you hang up on me twice in a row, you miserable son of a bitch, when all I am trying to do is help you? You—

Oh, hello, Stewart, I'm sorry. Welcome back. No, it's—
Congratulations for what?

Yes, it's been an interesting few weeks, they got rid of Diem all right, but not "just like I told them to," Stew. If you think I have that sort of influence on the South Vietnamese generals, I can only say I'm flattered.

What about the White House?

Oh please. I *told* them no such thing, and they *did* no such thing.

Well, even if we merely looked the other way while that very unpleasant man was removed—

All right, was "killed." Don't be prissy, Stewart, this isn't a Girl Scout picnic. The point is, Jack had the guts, thank God, to either arrange, or allow to occur, the necessary change in leadership, and now finally our responsibility is clear, and the *way* is clear for real success over there.

Balls.

He is *not* looking for an excuse to get out. That is a ludicrous misreading of both the situation and the man. Promise me you won't write that anywhere, you'll just embarrass yourself. He's far more tough-minded than you give him credit for, or than you yourself seem to be at the moment, if you don't mind my saying so.

Fine, I'll set you straight over dinner. Love to Tish.
(*He hangs up.* ABIGAIL *comes in, coat on, still wearing the skirt.*)

ABIGAIL: She said I could wear it.

JOE: I disapprove.

(*She folds her arms. He picks up a piece of paper.*)

JOE: "Courage; vivacity."

ABIGAIL: *Animus.*

JOE: "To uncover or lay bare."

(*She giggles. He rolls his eyes.*)

ABIGAIL: *Aperio.*

JOE: Yes. "Grasping, or obstinate."

ABIGAIL: *Tenax?*

JOE: Good. "Immortal." Too easy.

ABIGAIL: *Immortalis.*

JOE: "Evasiveness."

ABIGAIL: Ter . . . *shit!*

JOE: Or "reluctance" . . .

ABIGAIL: *Tergiversatio!*

JOE: Bravo. Finally: how fitting. "Skilled, expert."

ABIGAIL: *Peritus.*

JOE: Satisfactory. Go and flaunt yourself in the streets.

(ABIGAIL *goes.*)

Abigail.

(*She stops. He takes out his wallet and gives her a few bills.*)

For an extra . . . Pepsi-Cola, or pizza, or whatever you kids are eating. And take a cab home.

ABIGAIL: Thanks, Joe.

(*She kisses him quickly on the cheek. The phone rings.* ABI-GAIL *exits.*)

JOE: Hello. Hello, Scotty. (*Pause.*) I accept your apology. Though I don't believe I've ever hung up on you.

Well, I don't recall any of that, but I appreciate your calling back. Nevertheless, I am right about this, Scotty, and you are wrong. I first went to Vietnam in 1954. *Nineteen fifty-four.* How long have your boys been over there? A year? Two years? Your *boys* scurry around out in the underbrush over there, interviewing every whining malcontent and defeatist in the army rank-and-file they can find, and calling their bitching and moaning the "truth," meanwhile all but calling the men at the top, the men in charge, the men who *know, liars*, and I call that undermining American interests, and I call it irresponsible and a stain on our profession—

No, I insist you hear me out. No, I listened to you, now it is my turn. And I am here to tell you for your own damn good to reassign them, or maybe you'd prefer to wait until after we lose Vietnam the way we lost China, and what comes next, tell me that? Yes, you're damn right I "subscribe" to the domino theory, I *named* the damned theory, and I'll—listen to me: the President thinks you should reassign them too. You bet your ass we spoke about it, and he agrees with me, and as soon as he gets back from Dallas I am going to urge him again to call you—I think it certainly *is* his goddamn

business, I don't know what on earth his business *is* if
not—

Pardon me, I have not only the *right* but the *obliga-
tion* to—oh, fuck you too.

(*He hangs up. Beat.* SUSAN MARY *enters.*)

SUSAN MARY: Joe—

JOE: (*Fury*) For Chrissake, *do you ever knock?*

SUSAN MARY: Joe.

(*He looks at her. She looks stricken. From off—a choked
sob from* ABIGAIL.)

JOE: Is that Abby? Is she all right? Did you two argue?

SUSAN MARY: Come into the living room.

JOE: Why? What's the matter? What's going on?

SUSAN MARY: It's . . . You need to come look at the
television.

(JOE *gets up and follows her from the room. The phone begins to ring.*)

fade

SCENE 5

JOE's *study. That night.* JOE *typing.* STEWART *writing on a yellow pad.* JOE *finishes, takes the page out of the typewriter, and hands it to* STEWART. *He reads.*

STEWART: Damn it. I'm gonna bawl like a baby.

JOE: It's not that good.

STEWART: "The worthy citizen of a nation great and free—a nation, as he liked to think, that is great because it is free, and this was the thought that always inspired his too brief leadership of this republic."

It's good.

JOE: It can be improved.

STEWART: Maybe. Third graf.

JOE: Third, fourth, and fifth, I should think.

STEWART: Nah, don't touch the fifth.

JOE: Let me see yours.

STEWART: I got nothing.

JOE: Let me see. (STEWART *shows him the pad.*) No, you really don't have anything, do you?

STEWART: I shouldn't have come over here.

JOE: I'm glad you did. Sit down. Do you want to use my portable?

STEWART: I should get home. The kids were hysterical. They don't understand what's going on, but they see everybody in tears, so they're a mess too.

JOE: Have them all come over here. Is Tish all right?

STEWART: She's a rock. She's having anyone who wants to come. Feeding the whole neighborhood. Nobody wants to be alone tonight. And my editor wants a profile of Johnson by tomorrow morning.

JOE: So?

STEWART: I can't work tonight.

JOE: Nonsense. On a night like this, there's nothing you can do but work.

(*He puts another sheet of paper into the typewriter and begins typing.* SUSAN MARY *comes in with coffee.*)

SUSAN MARY: I gave Jose and Maria the night off. And to-morrow too.

JOE: That's fine.

STEWART: How's Abigail?

SUSAN MARY: She went out. There's some sort of vigil form-ing on the Mall. I thought it was right to let her go.

STEWART: How are you?

SUSAN MARY: I can't stop this ridiculous crying. (*She wells up.*) Damn it. There I go again.

(JOE *holds out a handkerchief without looking up from his typewriter.* STEWART *hands her one too.* STEWART's *is closer.* SUSAN MARY *takes it.* STEWART *puts an arm around her to comfort her. She falls into his arms, holding him very tightly, needing this.* STEWART *is surprised.* JOE *doesn't look up.* SUSAN MARY *collects herself, pulls away.*)

SUSAN MARY: I feel so useless. I can't stand this doing nothing. I was in France after the war. I helped the Red Cross, we had *responsibilities*. I helped people find their families after they'd come out of the camps . . . I was good at it. I can't watch any more television. The goddamn television, I hate it. I've called all my friends on the phone. I can't stand hearing their dead voices.

JOE: We must all try to keep busy in the coming weeks and months.

SUSAN MARY: I don't want to be busy, I want to be necessary.

JOE: But since you are not, you must try to occupy yourself somehow.

(*Beat. She stares at him.*)

SUSAN MARY: I'm going out.

JOE: Where?

SUSAN MARY: To find Abby.

JOE: You'll never find her. There'll be thousands.

SUSAN MARY: That's not the point. I want to be there.

STEWART: Maybe I'll go too.

JOE: You have work to do.

STEWART: It is work. It's something happening. I should see it. (*To* SUSAN MARY) Do you mind if we swing by the house? I want to take my kids.

SUSAN MARY: Of course not.

JOE: They're too young.

STEWART: I want them to be there. No. I just want them with me. (*Beat.*) You should come too.

JOE: I have work to do. (*He keeps typing.*)

STEWART: All right. (*Beat.*) I'll call you later, Joe.

JOE: Please.

(STEWART *looks at him, then exits. Beat.* SUSAN MARY *looks at* JOE.)

SUSAN MARY: Joe?

JOE: Yes?

SUSAN MARY: Stop typing. (JOE *stops. Beat.*) Are you all right?

JOE: Yes.

SUSAN MARY: He was also your friend.

JOE: I don't have time to think about that right now.

SUSAN MARY: Will you come with us? (*He shakes his head.*) Joe . . .

(*She goes to him. Tries to embrace him. He lets her, briefly, then pulls away.* SUSAN MARY *moves away. She exits.* JOE *starts to change pages in his typewriter. Sees the handkerchief and starts to put it back in his pocket. Suddenly lets out a single sob. Swallows it. Then carefully wipes his face, folds the handkerchief. He puts another page in the typewriter and begins typing again, with greater intensity.*)

End of Act One

ACT TWO

SCENE 1

New York, 1965. An auditorium, backstage. HALBERSTAM *studying some papers.* STEWART *enters.*

HALBERSTAM: Hello. This is a surprise. To what do I owe the— Are you coming to my talk? I'm honored.

STEWART: No. I need to speak with you.

HALBERSTAM: Well. We could get a drink after, I guess.

STEWART: No, now. Your talk can wait.

(*Beat.*)

HALBERSTAM: No it can't. Excuse me.

STEWART: David.

HALBERSTAM: *Excuse me.* You're welcome to go out front and listen. I'll be taking questions after.

STEWART: I got your package.

(*Beat.*)

HALBERSTAM: I'm sorry?

STEWART: That was a goddamn shitty thing to do. Is that how you people do things now? Is this how you prove a point?

HALBERSTAM: What?

STEWART: You couldn't go ahead and send it straight to me?

A friend at the AP brought me his. He took me to lunch, he didn't know what to say, he's a churchgoing man, he was *mortified*. You put him in a terrible position. I thought a lot of things about you, David, but I didn't think you were a coward. You should have had the guts to put your name on it.

HALBERSTAM: I have no idea what you're talking about, Stewart.

STEWART: Bullshit. You ought to be ashamed of yourself. You set yourself up as some sort of righteous, truth-telling . . . it turns my stomach. These kids out there might fall for it, but I don't. Shame on you.

(STEWART *starts to go.*)

HALBERSTAM: Stewart.

(STEWART *stops.*)

Is this about the . . . your brother's . . .

(STEWART *stares at him.*)

They didn't come from me.

STEWART: Who, then?

HALBERSTAM: I don't know.

STEWART: I don't believe you.

HALBERSTAM: Fine, but I got a set too.

(*Beat.*)

STEWART: You did.

HALBERSTAM: Four or five guys got sent the package. That I know of. How many do you—

STEWART: Three.

HALBERSTAM: Yeah, they're really circulating.

STEWART: Who sent them, David?

HALBERSTAM: I told you, I don't know. How the hell should I know? Why would you think it was me?

STEWART: Or one of your cohorts. To . . . show me. To prove a point.

HALBERSTAM: What point?

STEWART: That what you told me in Saigon about Joe was true.

HALBERSTAM: You knew it was true.

(*Beat.*)

STEWART: All right. Then . . . to push back. Against Joe. A warning shot.

HALBERSTAM: Now, that makes a little more sense. But no. I don't think so. Come on. Give us a little more credit.

STEWART: I'd like to.

HALBERSTAM: No one I know had even seen the photographs before a few days ago.

STEWART: That's not what you told me in Saigon. You said you knew people who had seen them.

HALBERSTAM: Okay, so I was exaggerating a little bit. There were rumors, but it was just guys winding each other up. Like those stories in high school about the cheerleader and the whole football team. Somehow you never actually met anyone with firsthand knowledge.

STEWART: Not anymore.

(*Beat.*)

HALBERSTAM: Yeah, well, I think you owe me an apology. You barge in here, I'm about to give a speech—

STEWART: I'm sorry. (*Beat.*) Who do you think sent them out?

HALBERSTAM: Well, who had them? I dunno. The Russians, I guess?

STEWART: (*Mock-dramatic*) The *KGB*.

HALBERSTAM: I know. Or our guys? I just don't know.

STEWART: Not our guys.

HALBERSTAM: Why not?

STEWART: Who?

HALBERSTAM: FBI? CIA?

STEWART: No. How would they have obtained them, to begin with.

HALBERSTAM: Lots of ways.

STEWART: What would be the point of throwing them around?

HALBERSTAM: Maybe the administration asked them to.

STEWART: Oh, don't be ridiculous.

HALBERSTAM: I've been reading your brother's stuff, Stewart. I doubt very much that Johnson enjoys being called a bed-wetting pinko sissy-boy every time he utters a halfway sensible word about Vietnam. Joe's really pushing it. He's taunting him. He's really lost it since JFK died. I used to enjoy reading his stuff. No, I did. I mean, I despised every word, but there was real skill there, real finesse. Now it's just piss and venom. I don't know who *wouldn't* want to knock him down at this point, to be honest. (*Beat.*) You look terrible.

STEWART: My cares are resting heavily upon me.

HALBERSTAM: No, I mean it. You don't look good.

STEWART: Fuck you.

HALBERSTAM: You want a cigarette?

STEWART: Yeah, all right.

(HALBERSTAM *gives him one and lights it.* STEWART *drags, studies it.*)

I don't know what to tell him.

HALBERSTAM: About what?

STEWART: The pictures getting around.

HALBERSTAM: He doesn't *know*?

STEWART: No. And he *won't*. Not if I can help it. It would kill him. It would just play into his paranoia. And his family . . . Don't . . . make it any worse, all right? Talk to your friends?

(*Beat.*)

HALBERSTAM: I'll see what I can do.

STEWART: Thank you.

HALBERSTAM: Don't thank me. Whatever you think of the younger generation, we're not sleaze merchants.

STEWART: I know that. (*Beat.*) By the way. Congratulations. On the prize.

HALBERSTAM: It's all downhill from here.

STEWART: I doubt that very much. (*He takes a long drag.*) I've always . . . coveted it.

HALBERSTAM: It's not too late for you, Stew.

STEWART: (*Light*) I think it may be, actually.

HALBERSTAM: I have to go on. (STEWART *nods.* HALBER-STAM *starts off.*) Stay and listen. You might learn something.

fade

SCENE 2

JOE's *study. November 1965.* JOE *typing.* SUSAN MARY *opens the door.*

JOE: Working.

SUSAN MARY: You said after the last one, you always want to approve the seating plan.

(JOE *keeps typing;* SUSAN MARY *waits impatiently.*)

SUSAN MARY: Joe. Do you—

JOE: Read me the list.

SUSAN MARY: Robert McNamara and wife.

JOE: All right.

SUSAN MARY: The Achesons.

JOE: Good.

SUSAN MARY: Two senators. Fulbright and Church.

JOE: Church is a bore.

SUSAN MARY: His wife is lovely.

JOE: So together they make half a bore. How many are we having? Ten? I guess we can afford half. Barely.

SUSAN MARY: Stewart and Tish.

JOE: Yes.

SUSAN MARY: And Abigail . . .

JOE: You didn't tell me she was coming.

SUSAN MARY: Joe, I did, she has her winter break, she's taking the train down from Boston today.

JOE: You never said anything.

SUSAN MARY: I told you a dozen times. You weren't paying attention.

JOE: I wouldn't have scheduled a dinner if I'd known she was coming back today.

SUSAN MARY: Of course you would have.

JOE: Well, I would have invited another guest at least. Now we have an odd number. Who are we going to put her next to?

SUSAN MARY: It's all right. She's bringing a friend, she said.

JOE: To stay?

SUSAN MARY: Yes. Just for the vacation.

JOE: Oh, for God's sake, Susan, this isn't a flophouse.

SUSAN MARY: It's only for a week or so.

JOE: There isn't a spare room. I don't want anybody on the couch. I'll have to tiptoe by her going into breakfast. The girl will have to sleep in Abigail's room. They can double up, I suppose . . .

SUSAN MARY: It's not a girl.

JOE: Really?

(SUSAN MARY *shakes her head.*)

JOE: A boyfriend?

SUSAN MARY: She hasn't used the word, but I suppose yes, he must be.

JOE: Are they sleeping together?

SUSAN MARY: How on earth should I know?

JOE: You don't talk about these things with your daughter?

SUSAN MARY: No.

JOE: Is she a virgin?

SUSAN MARY: Joe.

JOE: What?

SUSAN MARY: Don't be prurient.

JOE: It's not prurient, it's parental. Don't tell me you've never wondered.

SUSAN MARY: I don't know. I've always assumed she was—

JOE: Oh, that's absurd. She's eighteen years old. Surely she's sleeping with this boy. Even in our era, perfectly decent girls were experienced fornicators by her age, and young people today are far more wanton.

SUSAN MARY: I don't even want to think about it.

JOE: Well, now we have to think about it. Do we let them share a room? Astounding that we're even asking the question. Social mores have broken down so completely . . .

SUSAN MARY: Then let's just put him on the couch and be done with it.

JOE: If we put him on the couch, he'll be sneaking into her room in the middle of the night, bumping into furniture, keeping everyone awake . . .

SUSAN MARY: So what, then? I just put him in her room, say "Good night, have at it"? I'd have to look at them at breakfast—

JOE: It is a dilemma. And what will the servants think?

SUSAN MARY: Please. You decide. It's your house.

JOE: It's your daughter. And it's your house too—

SUSAN MARY: (*Dismissive sound.*)

JOE: What?

SUSAN MARY: Nothing.

JOE: Go on, you were about to say something.

SUSAN MARY: I just . . . In four years here I haven't bought a piece of furniture, or a *dish* . . . hung a picture on a wall . . .

JOE: Susan. If you're unhappy with the decor, by all means, change it.

SUSAN MARY: I'm not unhappy with the decor. That's not the—

JOE: I've put considerable care into the place, and never actually had my taste questioned before—

SUSAN MARY: Your *taste* is *impeccable*, Joe, you know I—

JOE: But if you think you can do better—

SUSAN MARY: I don't. I just—I never think of this as *my* house, is all I—

JOE: Surely that is your failing, not mine.

(*Beat.*)

SUSAN MARY: (*Flat*) Surely it is.

JOE: I put an entire addition on the house just for you. Your room. It's what you said you wanted.

SUSAN MARY: I know. It's not your fault.

JOE: Evidently it is.

SUSAN MARY: No. You did everything right. I—

JOE: You said you needed your own room . . .

SUSAN MARY: I didn't. That wasn't—

JOE: You *didn't*? I don't see how I could possibly have misunderstood that; for God's sake, we looked at the architect's drawings together.

SUSAN MARY: Joe! I didn't want my own *room*, I wanted—

JOE: What?

SUSAN MARY: Never mind. Let's drop it.

JOE: You began it.

SUSAN MARY: It's my fault. I thought I didn't care about . . . all that. And I don't, really. I've never been one of those people who really needs that. Not even in my first marriage. I mean, it was perfectly nice, but after the children . . . And so I thought with you it wouldn't matter, that it might even be a relief not to . . .

But it is a *marriage*. And without the physical . . . element . . .

JOE: Without sex. Is that what you mean?

SUSAN MARY: Yes, of course.

JOE: You can say "sex," can't you?

SUSAN MARY: Yes.

JOE: Shall we review the whole vocabulary set? Intercourse, fucking, erection, balls, cock, tits, cunt.

SUSAN MARY: Stop it.

JOE: I told you when I proposed what my situation was.

SUSAN MARY: I know. You were very honest.

JOE: You said you understood.

SUSAN MARY: I did. I do.

JOE: Then what is the problem?

SUSAN MARY: I thought it would change.

JOE: *It*, madam?

SUSAN MARY: Your . . . nature. I thought I could . . .

JOE: Oh, Susan, for God's sake.

SUSAN MARY: What?

JOE: Don't humiliate yourself.

SUSAN MARY: I'm trying to explain to you—

JOE: You thought what, exactly? That your feminine *wiles* . . . your Mata Hari–like erotic aura . . . the pulsing electric charge of your sensuality would magnetically flip the poles of my *nature*, as you call it? Dear God, woman. You're attractive enough, but there are limits.

SUSAN MARY: Why do you have to be such a bastard?

JOE: Why do you have to be such a child? You knew exactly who I was because I was honest and I *told* you. You said yes anyway, because, you said, you loved me, and you wanted the life I could give you. And important men came to your dinner parties. And they're still coming. They're coming tonight, you'd better go get ready.

(*She starts to go, in tears.*)

And do put the young man in with your daughter; you're so concerned there's too little fucking in our house.

(SUSAN MARY *slaps him. Beat.*)

JOE: That was unforgivable.

(*Beat.*)

I haven't been myself lately.

SUSAN MARY: Lately.

JOE: I'm sorry.

SUSAN MARY: It's been two years since Dallas.

(*Beat.*)

JOE: I feel like my life has been broken in half. I don't enjoy anything anymore. Not the town. Not the work. Not even the damned parties. I—

(*A tap at the door.* STEWART *enters.*)

STEWART: Hello.

(JOE *quickly resumes work.*)

Working late?

JOE: I've been trying to finish a column, but there have been a number of distractions.

STEWART: I haven't seen you for a few weeks. I thought I'd say hello to my brother and sister-in-law before the company came. If you mind, I'll go walk around the damn block.

SUSAN MARY: Of course we don't mind. Hello, Stewart.

JOE: (*Grim*) I am in need of a drink.

SUSAN MARY: I'll get it.

JOE: I can get my own.

(JOE *exits.*)

STEWART: Maybe it's not a good time.

SUSAN MARY: (*Wiping her eyes*) No, it's fine. We just . . .

(*Beat.* STEWART *looks at her.*)

STEWART: Tish claims she's got a suitcase all ready to go in the front hall closet, just in case. I'm pretty sure it's only a prop. Never had the nerve to check inside, though. Keeps me in line.

Maybe you should try it.

SUSAN MARY: Oh, mine is packed.

STEWART: That bad?

SUSAN MARY: No. Just the usual . . . squabbles. (*Attempt at brightness*) I have found myself looking at apartment listings, though. Glancing, really. Just for fun. They're putting up that new complex, the enormous one, have you seen it?

STEWART: Those are gonna be the ugliest buildings in Washington.

SUSAN MARY: Supposed to be awfully nice inside. Some of my friends are looking at places there. I wouldn't mind living somewhere new; I've always lived in old houses.

STEWART: It'd be awfully quiet after the Center of the Universe.

SUSAN MARY: "Quiet and obscure" sounds all right to me sometimes.

(*He looks at her.*)

SUSAN MARY: I'm joking, Stewart, don't look so "concerned."

STEWART: I'm not.

SUSAN MARY: Good. Now. How was the last test?

STEWART: Ugh. Tish?

SUSAN MARY: Of course. She keeps me posted.

STEWART: I told her to keep it quiet.

SUSAN MARY: From me? That's absurd.

STEWART: What about—(*Indicates Joe.*)

SUSAN MARY: Never, not unless you give the word, you know that. What have you found out?

STEWART: Nothing.

SUSAN MARY: Still?

STEWART: They have no idea what it is. If it's really any-thing. They're useless. They've been running the damn tests for nearly a year. I think it's all a lot of bullshit, actually.

SUSAN MARY: Let's hope so.

STEWART: I can't believe she *updates* you.

SUSAN MARY: I ask her to. Maybe you should say something to Joe. He'd be upset if he got wind of it somehow and you hadn't mentioned anything . . .

STEWART: Not yet.

SUSAN MARY: Why not? He can be very understanding, when he—

(*She stops. They laugh together. Beat.*)

Anyway, he's your brother.

STEWART: Yeah, and I don't want his sympathy.

(*This is a slip. Beat.*)

SUSAN MARY: So. They think it might be something that will . . . require sympathy.

(*Beat.*)

STEWART: Yes.

(*Beat.*)

SUSAN MARY: Oh.

(*She embraces him, really shocked. She kisses his face. Then, surprising herself, his mouth. STEWART gently moves her away.*)

STEWART: No. No.

(*Beat.*)

SUSAN MARY: I'm sorry.

STEWART: They're not sure of anything.

(*She nods.* JOE *enters.* SUSAN MARY *leaves quickly.*)

JOE: She's irritable tonight.

STEWART: Mmm.

(JOE *goes back to his desk.*)

Haven't seen you since I got back from New York.

JOE: How was New York?

STEWART: Fine. How was Vietnam?

JOE: That was a month and a half ago. Fine.

(*Beat.*)

STEWART: How many times have you been this year?

JOE: Twice.

STEWART: I need to get back. I haven't been since, God, '63.

JOE: You're still busy with your civil rights things?

STEWART: Yes. Believe it or not, that issue's not quite re-
solved yet.

JOE: And how are the poor Negroes doing?

STEWART: Read my pieces.

JOE: I'm a little behind in my reading.

STEWART: I'm not.

(*Beat.*)

You've been pretty tough on Johnson lately.

JOE: LBJ is a complicated fellow. He's physically intimidat-
ing but surprisingly sensitive to public accusations of
weakness. It's been interesting testing the limits of his
vulnerability.

STEWART: A little experiment.

JOE: He will do the right thing on Vietnam if I have anything to say about it. And I have a great deal to say about it.

STEWART: Did you read Lippmann last week?

JOE: No.

STEWART: "If Johnson continues to escalate, at least 50 percent of the responsibility will be Joe Alsop's."

JOE: I would hope for at least that much.

(*Beat.*)

STEWART: I . . . went up to Columbia University while I was in New York. Pretty interesting.

JOE: Surveying the nation's youth?

STEWART: Just trying to keep my finger on the pulse.

JOE: For the *Post* or freelance?

STEWART: Freelance, if it turns into anything.

JOE: It sounds like a waste of time, frankly.

STEWART: (*Ignoring this*) Some of these kids, you can't believe the stuff they're wearing now.

JOE: I've seen pictures.

STEWART: Like a gypsy circus. You can't tell the boys from the girls sometimes. Some of the boys are better-looking, actually.

JOE: Oh dear. You're not turning fairy on us, are you, Stewart?

STEWART: (*Mild*) No.

(*Beat.*)

I heard David Halberstam speak.

JOE: Hmm.

STEWART: He raked us over the coals.

JOE: Us?

STEWART: He used us as an example of what's wrong with "elite opinion." He used the name Alsop as a kind of punch line. The dying WASP elite, he called us. The audience clapped, and laughed.

JOE: I'm glad they enjoyed themselves.

STEWART: They call us "the Establishment."

JOE: Well, that's good, anyway.

STEWART: It's not a compliment.

(*Beat.*)

Halberstam—

JOE: Halberstam is pursuing a personal vendetta, because he believes that a year ago I tried to get him fired.

STEWART: Did you?

JOE: Yes.

STEWART: Why?

JOE: Why? What do you mean, why? Because he's a defeatist and a disgrace to the profession.

STEWART: Jesus, Joe.

JOE: What?

STEWART: Who the hell do you think you are?

JOE: I know who *I* am. It's you I'm worried about. What on earth has gotten into you, Stewart? Listening to *college students*? Since when do you give two shits about the so-called *opinions*—i.e., the knee-jerk juvenile *fancies*—of a bunch of long-haired teenage radicals? I certainly don't. They don't know politics. They don't know history. They don't know *anything*. We don't write for them.

STEWART: Who do we write for?

JOE: The influential.

STEWART: You think those kids aren't influential? Have you visited the campuses lately?

JOE: No, I haven't been hanging around on college campuses, Stewart. I've been rather busy in some other places. Vietnam, for example.

STEWART: What did you see in Vietnam?

JOE: I saw brave kids risking their lives. I saw the endlessly resourceful military of a great and benevolent power in a twilight struggle for freedom against an inhuman enemy.

STEWART: Save that crap for the column. What did you really see?

JOE: The implication that I'd present a different picture to my brother in private than I would to my readers is deeply offensive to me.

STEWART: Did you get out in the field?

JOE: Of course I was out in the field. I *live* in the field. What are you *implying*, Stewart?

STEWART: I'm just saying. Halberstam, Sheehan, those guys, they're young guys and they're hotheaded but they're smart and they're good—

JOE: They are *children*. They're in their *twenties*—

STEWART: They're professionals, Joe, just like we were professionals in *our* twenties, and they've been there for a pretty decent spell. And they don't want America to lose.

JOE: They very definitely *do* want America to lose.

STEWART: Oh, come on. You can't believe that.

JOE: Have you seen the coverage? (*Suddenly shouting*) Have you read the *fucking* stories?

STEWART: Easy, Joe . . .

JOE: I have just been going through the reports from Ia Drang. It's the subject of my next column. Do you know *anything at all* about Ia Drang?

STEWART: Of course I do. Don't shout at me.

JOE: Four hundred fifty Air Cav soldiers surrounded in a valley by over two thousand North Vietnamese. *Two thousand.* Against our *four hundred fifty.* And we fight our way out. Two hundred fifty Americans killed. Heartbreaking. Heartbreaking. But—

We killed *one thousand* North Vietnamese Communist troops. My sources at the Pentagon say probably more. We *routed* them. We *obliterated* a massively superior force by a factor of *one half.* It was *astonishing.* It was *heroic.*

And *Sheehan*—do you want to know what he writes?

"American casualties . . . Americans' heaviest *death toll* . . . serious *losses* . . ."

STEWART: What would you call a 50 percent casualty rate?

JOE: We killed them by a factor of seven to one. *Seven to one.* I call that a massive victory. Would it have killed him to use the word *victory*? I think it would. Or *success* or *won*?

STEWART: I don't know. I don't know, Joe. I wish I had your certainty.

JOE: What is there to be uncertain about? A victory is a victory.

STEWART: Except when it's not.

JOE: *Except*, I suppose you mean, when certain correspondents *say* it's not, and the American people, who have no better source of information, *believe* them.

STEWART: So you'll be the better source of information.

JOE: *General Westmoreland* is the better source. *Robert McNamara*. What better sources do you need? For God's sake, don't expertise and authority mean anything anymore? I have to stand up for these men and the damned hard work they do and for the *simple truth*, which they have maintained steadily, *courageously*, for many months, through sunny days and stormy, which is that we *must* win this war, we *will* win it, and *we are winning it now*.

STEWART: I heard Westmoreland's gonna ask for a hundred thousand more troops in 1966.

JOE: I believe that is more or less correct.

STEWART: How come we need a hundred thousand more kids if we're winning now?

JOE: Do you want a debate, Stew? Is that what you want?

STEWART: What's the point? You don't listen to me. You don't listen to anyone. I don't know why you bother to go on these trips. You never change your mind, and you sit with the same old fossils peddling the same old crap—

JOE: Oh, this is spite. This is just sheer professional envy.

STEWART: It's my name, not just yours. The Alsop *brothers*—

JOE: I won't be blamed for sharing a name with you.

STEWART: We're linked whether we want it or not, and I'm not gonna sit here at the end and watch you fuck up everything—

JOE: The *end*? The *end* of what? Nothing's at an *end*. Don't blame me because you're floundering in your career.

STEWART: I—

JOE: You could have stayed with me, you could have stayed with the column! I would have *helped* you. I'm helping you *now*. My damn *name, my* name, is all that's keeping *you* afloat.

STEWART: I don't want your help and I don't need your goddamn help, you reckless arrogant prick.

JOE: "Reckless"?

STEWART: I—

JOE: Now, arrogant I will accept, and the other too, gladly, but I have never been *reckless* in my *life*—

STEWART: Oh, come on, Joe. You've taken so many idiotic risks it's a miracle it hasn't all blown up in your face. Half the time when we were partners I was terrified that— I never said anything. It's none of my business how you run your life—

JOE: Just a moment. I thought we were talking about work. What does my "life" have to do with anything?

STEWART: It's—nothing. I'm sorry I said it.

JOE: Blown up in my face? What the hell do you think you're talking about?

STEWART: Nothing. Look, forget it. See you at dinner.

JOE: Stewart.

(*Beat.*)

STEWART: Moscow.

JOE: Moscow?

(*Beat.*)

STEWART: Shit. Oh, the hell with it. Never mind.

(*Beat.*)

JOE: (*Calm*) No. You've obviously heard certain rather scurrilous rumors. Ugly words, "blackmail," and so forth . . . I'm not surprised. I know they're out there, of course. I wouldn't have thought my brother capable of believing them, let alone repeating them.

STEWART: Look, I—

JOE: Do you believe them?

(STEWART *says nothing.*)

JOE: Have you discussed them with my wife? I'm aware you're close.

STEWART: God no. Never.

JOE: Do you believe them?

(STEWART *looks away.*)

Stewart.

(*Beat.*)

I will *never* forgive you for this.

(*Beat. A knock on the door.* ABIGAIL *enters. With her is* PHILIP. *They both have a protohippie look.*)

ABIGAIL: Joe? Mom said you were— Oh, hi, Stewart.

STEWART: Hi.

ABIGAIL: I'd like you to meet my friend Phili—

(JOE *suddenly points to* PHILIP.)

JOE: *You.* Sit down here now.

PHILIP: I—

JOE: *Sit down.*

(PHILIP *sits.* JOE *makes a big show for* STEWART *of picking up a pad and pen and sits next to* PHILIP *on the couch.*) Now. I want you to tell me . . . and I'm going to write it *all down*—

What do you think about *everything*?

fade

SCENE 3

Winter 1967. Outside a church. HALBERSTAM *in an overcoat.* JOE *enters, sees him, stops. Beat.*

HALBERSTAM: I didn't expect the honor guard.

JOE: He was a soldier.

HALBERSTAM: I didn't know that.

JOE: He parachuted into occupied France. He was decorated for it.

(*Beat.*)

I didn't know you were friends.

HALBERSTAM: We weren't. We met a few times. He never mentioned it?

JOE: No.

(HALBERSTAM *takes this in.*)

HALBERSTAM: First time in Vietnam in . . . '63, I guess it was.

JOE: Ah.

HALBERSTAM: I'm afraid I sort of exploded at him.

JOE: Yes, you're famous for that.

HALBERSTAM: He took it incredibly well. He just sort of . . . *listened* to me. Like I was an interesting phenomenon.

Noteworthy, but not something to get emotional about. I just kept pushing . . . It was all I could do to get one "fuck you" out of him.

JOE: He was a reporter.

HALBERSTAM: Yeah. That's right.

JOE: He told me a few months ago, about his leukemia— "It's a very interesting experience. I just wish I weren't so personally involved."

(HALBERSTAM *smiles. Beat.*)

HALBERSTAM: Anyway. I'm sorry.

(*Beat.*)

JOE: I haven't seen your byline lately.

HALBERSTAM: I'm writing a book.

JOE: What about?

HALBERSTAM: How we got into this mess.

JOE: Do you have a title?

HALBERSTAM: Not yet.

JOE: Am I in it?

HALBERSTAM: I'm afraid you'll have to be.

JOE: Well. Spell my name correctly.

HALBERSTAM: Okay.

(*He turns to go.*)

JOE: David?

(HALBERSTAM *turns.*)

Thank you for coming.

(HALBERSTAM *nods, and exits.* ABIGAIL *has entered. Full hippie attire.* JOE *turns and sees her. He goes to her, very pleased.*)

JOE: Abby! I saw you in the church. I didn't think you'd be able to come.

ABIGAIL: It's good to see you, Joe.

JOE: My God, you look like Pocahontas. You should have called. You should have told me you were coming, I'd have picked you up at the station.

ABIGAIL: No, come on. You have too much going on.

JOE: Don't be ridiculous. Where are you staying?

ABIGAIL: I'm not.

JOE: What?

ABIGAIL: I've got to be back at school tomorrow. Exams.

JOE: You'll at least let me take you to dinner.

ABIGAIL: Can't. I'm taking the bus right back.

JOE: Oh, that's ridiculous.

ABIGAIL: I was lucky to get away at all. I wanted to make sure and say hi, though, before I—

JOE: Oh, come on. Lunch, at least? Please. Nothing elaborate, we'll go somewhere casual. (*Re: her clothes*) We'll have to, actually . . .

ABIGAIL: I'm sorry, Joe.

(JOE *swallows his disappointment.*)

JOE: No apologies. It means the world that you came at all.

ABIGAIL: I'm so sorry about Stewart.

JOE: Thank you.

(*Beat.*)

ABIGAIL: How are you?

JOE: Well, it wasn't entirely unexpected. After he told me, he still had . . . a few months. That helps a bit. But it's still difficult. The younger sibling is just not meant to predecease the older, you know, it just seems . . . poorly managed, somehow.

ABIGAIL: Uh-huh.

JOE: We were partners for two decades, and close our entire lives. Mostly. He would never admit it . . . and nobody but I saw it . . . but we complemented each other, I think.

ABIGAIL: No, I saw it.

JOE: You did?

ABIGAIL: That night a couple years ago. Remember? I was visiting from school?

JOE: Which?

ABIGAIL: I brought that boy over.

JOE: Yes. What was his name?

ABIGAIL: Philip.

JOE: That's right, Philip. Your boyfriend.

ABIGAIL: Well. Semi-.

JOE: What was wrong with him?

ABIGAIL: Nothing. He was very . . . mild. Anyway. You *terrorized* him. That interrogation.

JOE: I interviewed him.

ABIGAIL: You spent an *hour.* You buttonholed him, you *probed* him *mercilessly* for his opinions about the war, "today's youth," the whole geopolitical deal . . . He was a *piano teacher.* He was quaking.

JOE: His responses were reasonably cogent, as I recall.

ABIGAIL: Then we went in to dinner and he's sitting next to

Robert McNamara, and you repeat everything Philip said and make him repeat himself to the whole table, all those arrogant, articulate people, those professional talkers . . .

JOE: He didn't do as well there.

ABIGAIL: No. Stewart tried to defend him, though.

JOE: Yes, he did.

ABIGAIL: He took his side, backed him up all the way. I loved him for that.

JOE: Still. The prosecution, I believe, won. Did that have anything to do with why he didn't spend the night?

ABIGAIL: *Possibly*, Joe. Possibly.

JOE: Oh dear.

ABIGAIL: He took the next train back to Boston. He never spoke to me again.

JOE: Well, look, if I had known he was so sensitive—

(JOE *sees she's laughing.*)

It's good you can laugh about it now.

ABIGAIL: I don't know how Mom lived with you.

(*Beat.*)

JOE: How is she?

ABIGAIL: She's okay. Keeping busy.

JOE: I would have liked to see her here.

ABIGAIL: She wanted to come. She loved Stewart.

JOE: I know that.

ABIGAIL: She just . . . it's so soon after . . .

JOE: No. I understand. Tell her I wouldn't mind hearing from her.

ABIGAIL: No, Joe. She can't deal with all the legal stuff right now.

JOE: No, God no, I'm not trying to rush her along, it would be strictly for the sake of friendship.

We *were* friends, you know. Good friends. At the beginning. She kept me honest. Or tried, at least.

Stewart tried too. And in return I abused him.

ABIGAIL: I'm sure he didn't see it that way.

JOE: He saw everything clearly.

(*Beat.*)

I have no one.

(JOE *weeps.* ABIGAIL *tries to comfort him, awkwardly. Beat. He collects himself, dries his eyes with a handkerchief.*)

Oh dear. I'm sorry.

ABIGAIL: It's all right.

JOE: Abby, there's something I feel you should know. It might help you make sense of . . . I don't know, things, your youth, now that you're at an age when people try to take stock of their upbringing, understand their parents . . . I don't actually know if you ever considered me a *parent*, but I certainly consider *myself* . . .

ABIGAIL: Joe, of course, you know I do.

JOE: Yes, well, that's not even the point. The point is, you see, I'm not . . . your mother and I had a somewhat unconventional arrangement, and for a time at least a not unsuccessful one—or even particularly *unusual* one, I might add—but the fact remains that we . . . you see,

I—and I haven't spoken about this to very many people, just your mother and Stewart, really, and now they're . . . but you're, as I say, family, and I want you to know, you deserve to know that, that I . . .

ABIGAIL: Joe. I know.

JOE: You don't even know what it is I'm going to say.

ABIGAIL: Yes, I do.

JOE: She *told* you? I can't believe she—

ABIGAIL: No. God, no, she never *said* anything. Mom? Are you kidding? She didn't even say anything when I got my first period, she just sent me to her doctor in a chauffeured car. No. She didn't have to. I mean, it's pretty obvious. I think probably everybody knows.

JOE: (*Stunned by this*) Everybody?

ABIGAIL: Joe. It's really not that big a thing.

(*She hugs him. He returns it, awkward.*)

I have to go. My exam—

JOE: Yes, of course. What is it?

ABIGAIL: Oh, I have three or four, they really pile up.

JOE: If it's Latin, you don't have a thing to worry about.

ABIGAIL: It isn't Latin.

JOE: It isn't anything, Abby. It was my school, too. It isn't exam week. The term just started.

ABIGAIL: Yeah. I . . . dropped out. I wanted to work full-time. Against the war. I didn't think you'd want to hear that.

JOE: I see. No. I admire your . . . willingness to act on conviction, however misguided.

(Beat.)

Write?

(She nods, then starts to go.)

And if you run into him in Boston, say hello to poor Philip
for me.

(She smiles, briefly.)

ABIGAIL: I can't. He was drafted.

fade

SCENE 4

Washington. Summer 1968. The Mall. A bearded MAN *in his thirties, holding a magazine. Off, the sounds of a demonstration.* JOE *enters. He looks tired and irritated. He sits on a bench. The* MAN *eventually sits down too, nods to* JOE, *begins glancing at his magazine.*

JOE: There used to be places in Washington, D.C., where a man could sit and enjoy the afternoon without being subjected to *tribal drumming.*

MAN: They've been there all morning.

JOE: They've been there all year. My God. Don't they have anything better to do?

MAN: What's better to do?

JOE: Honest labor? Education? Travel? Auto-eroticism? *Anything's* better. The *chanting,* my God. You can't escape it. I can hear it in the library.

MAN: They're young. Students.

JOE: Do you know where students spent most of their time in my day? *In school.*

MAN: Yes.

JOE: It's a quaint idea, I know. But these . . . "hippies," or

"New Lefties," or SDS-ees, or whatever they're calling themselves this week, they don't have the slightest interest in—

(*He stops himself.*)

But now *I'm* disturbing *your* day. My apologies.

MAN: It's no problem.

(*Beat.* JOE *looks at him.*)

JOE: Say that again.

MAN: Sorry?

JOE: What you just said.

MAN: "It's no problem"?

(*Beat.*)

JOE: You are Russian.

MAN: Yes.

JOE: I knew it.

MAN: Well, Soviet.

JOE: I heard the faintest trace of it.

MAN: Damn.

JOE: What?

MAN: I worked hard to lose it. I pride myself on being completely unaccented.

JOE: Well, that's impossible. No one, however fluent—

MAN: I listen to tapes. I try to pick the best voice.

JOE: Unquestionably, the finest American speaking voice of my lifetime belonged to Franklin Delano Roosevelt.

MAN: Too WASPy.

JOE: I beg your pardon.

MAN: I listen to Walter Cronkite.

JOE: No one should listen to Walter Cronkite.

MAN: And Alistair Cooke, he has a nice quality.

JOE: Yes, I suppose he's all right.

(*Beat.*)

MAN: I like the way the English sound. I've gone back and forth. For a long time I couldn't decide who I wanted to sound like. I even considered Lennon.

JOE: Lenin?

MAN: No, John Lennon. (*Beatles voice*) "Those in the cheap seats applaud. The rest of you just rattle your jewelry."

(JOE *looks blank.*)

He's one of the Beatles.

JOE: Oh, the Beatles, yes. Thank God, that silly fad ran its course.

MAN: Are you joking? They're great artists.

JOE: What?

MAN: Have you heard *Sgt. Pepper's*?

JOE: What is that?

MAN: It's a record album by the Beatles.

JOE: Oh. No, I haven't heard it.

MAN: It came out a year ago.

JOE: I haven't even heard *of* it.

MAN: You're joking.

JOE: No.

MAN: It's brilliant! It's a symphony! How can you not have listened to it? It's like not having seen *Dr. Strangelove*.

JOE: I have my own doctor I'm very happy with.

MAN: You didn't see *Dr. Strangelove*?

JOE: I don't know who that is.

MAN: It's a film! With Peter Sellers! (*Imitates Strangelove pushing his arm down.*) "*Ja, mein Führer!*" He plays three roles! "You can't fight in here, this is the war room!" And George C. Scott, and Slim Pickens—"YEEEEHAAAAAW!"

JOE: Oh, yes, perhaps I have heard something about it. I don't go to the movies much. I saw the film of *My Fair Lady* a number of years ago, I enjoyed that.

MAN: (*Scorn*) *My Fair Lady. Strangelove* is the film. And *Sgt. Pepper!* I bought two so I can stack them on my turntable and don't have to get up and flip the record. Take my advice: buy two copies, get yourself a good pair of headphones, lie back, have a few glasses of wine—or something else—and you'll be transported. You'll blow your mind.

JOE: I don't think I'll be doing that.

MAN: Too bad.

(*Beat.*)

JOE: Tell me, how did you come here? Did you defect?

MAN: Defect? No, I work for the embassy.

JOE: You do?

MAN: Yes, I'm an attaché.

JOE: You certainly seem to have embraced the West.

MAN: The West will implode soon, a victim of its own internal contradictions, and the United States will be the first sucked into history's abyss.

JOE: Ah.

MAN: Meanwhile . . .

JOE: Yes?

MAN: Confidentially?

JOE: Please.

MAN: I love it here.

JOE: Really?

MAN: Ah, the music, the films, the food—breakfasts especially, the miracle of the "bottomless cup of coffee"!— the weather . . .

JOE: You love the weather in *Washington, D.C.*?

MAN: You've been to Moscow.

JOE: As a matter of fact, I have.

MAN: So you understand. And I love the bookstores . . . You can't imagine how it feels walking into an American bookstore. Or just a newsstand. The *magazines*—

JOE: What is that you're reading?

MAN: *Esquire.* Norman Mailer! Genius.

JOE: He's a thug.

MAN: No, he's fantastic, he's like something out of Dostoyevsky, a mad monk, hysterical and obscene, I love him. And James Baldwin. And Truman Capote and Paul Newman and James Brown and Andy Warhol.

JOE: Everyone you just named I frankly despise.

MAN: And those kids over there too.

JOE: Not all of them. My stepdaughter's in there somewhere, apparently. Her I like. The remaining 99.99 percent of that writhing, fetid mass, yes, with particular venom.

MAN: You know what? I think you hate America more than anyone at home does.

JOE: That's absurd. I love my country. I just don't care very much for many of the people in it right now.

(MAN *smiles. Beat.*)

JOE: Tell me, how exactly do your bosses at the embassy feel about your embrace of all things Western?

MAN: Not bosses. Comrades. (JOE *stares at him.*) And the top men I never deal with, and the mid-level officers are too busy buying hi-fis for their kids to listen to Simon and Garfunkel records to mind what we do in our spare time, as long as we behave sensibly during working hours, and don't . . .

(JOE *is still staring, frozen.*)

What?

(*Beat.*)

JOE: Andrei?

ANDREI: Yes.

JOE: My God. It's me, Joe. We met in Moscow. Ten years ago. You . . . came to my room.

ANDREI: (*Nods*) The columnist. I know. I was wondering when you'd . . .

JOE: What is it you want from me?

ANDREI: Nothing.

JOE: Please. This could hardly be an accidental meeting.

ANDREI: The embassy is there. You spend your mornings in the library. I see you here often, taking the air. It seemed silly never once to say hello. That's all.

JOE: Stop it. I'm not an idiot. Just tell me what you want and get it over with.

ANDREI: Only to say hello.

JOE: I don't believe you.

ANDREI: I guess I shouldn't be surprised. I read your work too. I never miss a column. You look for plots everywhere. Secret agendas.

JOE: And I usually find them.

ANDREI: Is it really so impossible to imagine I don't have one?

JOE: Yes.

ANDREI: How sad for you, then.

(*Beat.*)

JOE: You got your diplomatic posting.

ANDREI: Yes.

JOE: How is your sister? The . . . skier, wasn't she?

ANDREI: You have a remarkable memory. She is fine.

JOE: Really.

ANDREI: I've been able to help her since . . . my new job. I am trying to arrange for her to visit me here. It's not easy, but I'm close to getting permission. I want to take her to ski in Colorado. I think she would love the Rocky Mountains.

JOE: Congratulations. You've done well for yourself.

ANDREI: (*Noncommittal sound.*)

JOE: Quite a change from your wayward youth.

ANDREI: I don't think much about those days.

JOE: You entrapped me.

(*Beat.*)

ANDREI: It was just a job.

JOE: How many of those "jobs" did you do?

ANDREI: A few.

JOE: You were a contemptible little trick.

ANDREI: And you were procuring a whore. What did you expect?

JOE: I suppose now you're some sort of spy. "Attaché" indeed.

ANDREI: I *am* an attaché.

JOE: And what else?

ANDREI: Nothing else. A music fan.

JOE: Don't insult me. You were a tour guide working for the KGB, now you're an embassy aide and nothing else?

ANDREI: I never *worked* for them. If they asked, I did a job. A half a dozen times at most. If you think I had a choice, then you don't understand our system. I got out as soon as I could. I clawed my way into the diplomatic branch.

JOE: And they owed you after all the work you'd done.

ANDREI: It wasn't like that.

JOE: Oh, wasn't it.

ANDREI: I earned my way. I took *your* advice. I used my languages. In a way I owe this life to you.

JOE: That gives me such a warm feeling.

(ANDREI *stands.*)

ANDREI: I suppose . . . I just wanted to say thank you. And "I'm sorry," too. For any . . . distress I may have caused. Will you accept my apology?

JOE: If my feigned acceptance of your meaningless apology will send you faster on your way, gladly, and goodbye.

(JOE *puts out his hand, ironically.* ANDREI *takes it.*)

ANDREI: Didn't expect that much, actually. Perhaps you're going soft.

JOE: Perhaps.

(ANDREI *keeps holding* JOE's *hand.*)

ANDREI: It almost tempts me to ask you to dinner.

JOE: What?

ANDREI: In Moscow you said you always get the best tables. You could book it, and I could charge it to the Embassy.

(JOE *nearly laughs.*)

JOE: You haven't lost your gift for effrontery, I'll give you that. No. You got the handshake. Don't push your luck.

ANDREI: Too bad. (*Beat.*) Still. It's a beautiful afternoon, and I am here in this beautiful country. Thank you again.

(ANDREI *starts to go.*)

JOE: Andrei? Wait.

(ANDREI *stops.*)

It's I who should be thanking you.

ANDREI: For what?

(*Beat.*)

JOE: It's not every day a subject for a column drops into one's lap. I'd been struggling to find something for the next one, and now you've come to my rescue.

ANDREI: I don't understand.

JOE: "The new Soviet hypocrites." "A chance encounter on a

park bench with—we'll just call him 'Andrei'—gave me new hope for America's not-so-distant triumph in the Cold War . . . Seduced by the very pleasures of the West they claim to hate, these 'decadent-niks'"— something like that—"are secretly longing not for Stalingrad but for San Francisco" . . . it'll write itself. Not many do. I'm in your debt.

(*Beat.*)

ANDREI: You can't.

JOE: Don't be silly, you've given me a splendid idea for the sort of piece that will be talked of all over town. Do you imagine I'm going to pass it up?

ANDREI: They'll know it's me.

JOE: Not necessarily.

ANDREI: Of course they will.

JOE: I'll only use your first name, A-N-D-R-E-I. And don't worry, I won't say anything that isn't scrupulously accurate. I liked the bit about your bosses buying hi-fis, for example.

ANDREI: Please. I'll lose my job. I'll be ruined, humiliated—

JOE: (*Shouts*) Don't talk to me about humiliation!

ANDREI: I'm *sorry*. Should I say it again? I'm sorry about Moscow.

JOE: Fuck Moscow! I don't care about Moscow! You did your worst there and you didn't lay a *glove* on me. Do you know what I did with those ridiculous photographs those thugs who came to my door showed me? I took them straight to our ambassador. Then I went to the

FBI, and the State Department. I said, Here it is. Here's what I've done. Here's what I am. If my career's to end, I want *you* to end it, not those depraved blackmailing psychopaths over there. And they *didn't* end it. And *that* is the difference between my country and yours. You see? And then you tried *again*—don't think I don't know you scattered your photographic filth around Washington a few years ago, trying to frighten me, shame me before my enemies and friends. But I will not be silenced and I will not be shamed. I know how to handle you people. Christ, you disgust me. You think you've got us beat. You think you've got us on the run in Vietnam, you've got our youth running riot in the streets, naked and stoned out of their minds, you think you're winning. Well, not while I'm around, thank you very much. If you don't think I won't go absolutely to the limit to defend what I hold dear you don't know me very well, and you don't know this country very well. Study the history! You thought you had us fixed with Cuba, but JFK, a better man *by far* than any your country has ever produced, *outfoxed* you, God bless his soul, and then after Dallas you probably thought you'd caught another break—maybe you were *involved* with Dallas—I scoffed at that at the time but now I'm not so sure—and you surely thought LBJ, the big dumb cowboy, would go easy on you, but *I* bucked him up, by God, I stiffened his spine, and even if he's not man enough to finish the job, somebody else will. Nixon will, he will burn you bastards out of the jungles and *we will win* there, there and everywhere. God knows what miserable filthy tricks you'll stoop to next, but we will match you stunt for stunt and *we will win*. So fuck Moscow, and fuck *you*, sir. Fuck. You.

(*Beat.*)

ANDREI: I suppose I cannot stop you.

JOE: No, you cannot.

ANDREI: My sister—

(JOE *shrugs.* ANDREI *goes.* JOE *sits alone for a moment. Then slowly gets up. The set changes around him to his study.*)

SCENE 5

JOE's study. Night. JOE sits at his typewriter. He types purposefully for a bit. Then slows. Then stops.

He pulls the paper out of the typewriter and reads what he's written. A long pause. Then he violently crumples the paper and tears it.

He takes a breath.

He picks up the phone, dials.

JOE: Hello. It's Alsop. The column tomorrow is going to be a bit late. I'm sorry, I just wanted to let you know.

Yes, I thought I had a piece but I've changed my mind. It wasn't working. No, I know I've never been late before. I haven't been late in twenty-five years. That's precisely why you shouldn't be complaining now. I—

Yes, I have other ideas; I have a *thousand* ideas for Chrissake, don't worry. I'll get you something. Yes. All right.

(He hangs up. He puts another sheet of paper in the typewriter. He stares at it. He doesn't move. A moment.)

Curtain

Printed in the USA
CPSIA information can be obtained
at www.ICGtesting.com
LVHW091147150724
785511LV00005B/594